Dancing Shapes with Attitude

Ballet and Body Awareness for Young Dancers

Book Four in the Dancing Shapes Series

Dancing Shapes with Attitude

© 2021 *Once Upon a Dance*

All 2021 book sales donated to ballet companies struggling under COVID-19.

All rights reserved.
No part of this publication may be reproduced, distributed, or transmitted in any form or
by any means, including photocopying, without the prior written permission of the publisher,
except in the case of brief quotations and other noncommercial uses permitted by copyright law.
Dance teachers are welcome to use images for class instruction; please give the Dancing Shapes series credit.

Summary: This fourth *Dancing Shapes* volume presents an ongoing peek into one ballerina's journey,
discusses the subjectivity of dance, demonstrates *attitudes* and *arabesques,* and offers poses for aspiring dancers to re-create.

ISBN: 978-1-7365-8994-6 (Paperback); 978-1-7365-8995-3 (Hardcover); 978-1-7365-8996-0 (ebook)

JUVENILE NONFICTION: Performing Arts: Dance
(PERFORMING ARTS: Dance: Classical & Ballet; PERFORMING ARTS: Dance: Reference)

First Edition

All readers agree to release and hold harmless *Once Upon a Dance*
and all related parties from any claims, causes of action, or liability arising from the contents.
Use this book at your own risk.

Other *Once Upon a Dance* Titles:
Dancing Shapes: Ballet and Body Awareness for Young Dancers
More Dancing Shapes: Ballet and Body Awareness for Young Dancers
Nutcracker Dancing Shapes: Shapes and Stories from Konora's Twenty-Five Nutcracker Roles
Konora's Shapes: Poses from Dancing Shapes for Creative Movement & Ballet Teachers
More Konora's Shapes: Poses from More Dancing Shapes for Creative Movement & Ballet Teachers
Ballerina Dreams Ballet Inspiration Journal/Notebook
Dancing Shapes Ballet Inspiration Journal/Notebook
Joey Finds His Jump!: A Dance-It-Out Creative Movement Story for Young Movers
Petunia Perks Up: A Dance-It-Out Creative Movement and Meditation Story

Hello Fellow Dancer,

As usual, I have a lot to tell you, and I've crammed in a bunch of mini-chapters.

 The first section is about me and the ups and downs of trying to catch my dreams. *(page 6)*

 Some of those ups and downs were at ballet competitions. I'll share some of my experiences. *(page 12)*

 Please remember to warm up before dancing. *(page 19)*

 Next up, we'll talk ballet terms and explore different ways to pose our legs. *(page 20)*

 We'll make more complicated shapes, and I hope you'll enjoy the challenge of re-creating them. *(page 31)*

 If you want to learn more about the French ballet terms, there's a section at the end with translations. I call the ballet words *fancy French*. *(page 45)*

 I've left a few extra shapes on the opposite page for another time. I like to include duplicates from the story's pages so you can think about the details and whether you've seen them before. You might also recognize a couple poses from our other books.

So, are you ready to talk dance? Let's go!

Part One
About Me, Konora

Once Upon a Dance, it was December 2020. I had just auditioned for a company looking for a dancer to start in January. I'd made it to the final round and was wondering if I'd be moving to Missouri in a couple weeks.

Like many professions, ballet dancers often get hired long after they first apply. And, frequently, dancers audition multiple times before they're offered a job. Because companies might not have an opening for years, dancers sometimes have to wait, even when a company wants to hire them. Constant shifting is a common part of a ballet dancer's life.

The last three places I've danced, I wasn't invited until August and had to move and start in September. I applied with the Missouri company almost a year ago and only recently heard back. My parents never know where I'll be living, and planning is difficult.

Some folks who landed jobs in 2020 are still on a COVID-standby. But usually dancers manage to find something as things settle and people shift, and second company, apprentice, and trainee positions open up, even if it's not until late summer. It's a little stressful, though.

But with COVID, things are different, and I'm a little concerned the door might be closing on my ballet dreams. With most companies shut down for the year, my best shot at landing a job was canceled. Compared to many dancers, I got a late start deciding to try to make ballet my career, and a lot of dancers my age already have a job or have given up looking.

I started taking classes when I was practically a baby. I enjoyed ballet, but I reached the point where studios required more commitment. There were other things I loved doing, and I didn't want to spend that much time dancing. My mom, a believer in the benefits of ballet, called every studio in town and found one that would let me take class once a week. The irony was that two years later, I would be signed up for twelve classes a week!

At my ballet school, there were many performance opportunities. I got to portray so many fun and unique characters. The performance weekends we practically lived at the theater are some of my favorite memories. For some students, it wasn't their thing, and they decided not to participate in the shows. There are plenty of great things about studying ballet, even if you don't perform. If you've read my other books, you might guess what I'm going to say:

Dance is for everybody!

Thank you, Taylor, Elaina, and Emerald Ballet Theatre.

While I got to dance in many elegant costumes, it wasn't all tutus. What do you think of these pictures?

I enjoyed getting to dance evil or angry characters. Having a great attitude about every opportunity makes life and stage more fun for everyone. If the audience had to watch the same character over and over again, things would get pretty boring.

Left Photo: Sarah Jacobsen. Thank you, Elaina, Katie, and Clara.

Right Photo: Visual Arts Masters (VAM)

I'm not saying there weren't times I was disappointed with casting (who performs each role). Schools want to give many dancers the spotlight solo. After a chance at a lead role, students would move back to corps (group or backup). It makes sense to do it this way, but it wasn't always easy at the time. It helps to shake it off, do your best, and encourage your fellow dancers. I feel lucky we had supportive personalities in my level. It made that time in my life very special.

Thank you, friends and unknown photographer.

Part Two
Competitions and Opinions

Speaking of personalities: wow, would they come out at dance competitions! People seem to either love or hate competitions. My school participated in only one each year, which I thought was perfect.

We could join an ensemble dance with most of our class, and some students were chosen to work on solos, duets, or small group pieces. At my first competition, I think I was the only student not in pointe shoes in my age category, and my dance only lasted one minute. But I had fun!

Over the years, I saw kids and their families get caught up in the competitive mindset. Both parents and dancers would make decisions about whether to continue dancing based on the results of the competition. One year, a friend threw up backstage from the stress.

Looking back, I think not winning anything for several years helped me set realistic expectations, and I was able to have a more relaxed attitude.

The results were often surprising. We would all be sure someone would win top three, but they wouldn't even get top twelve. Or the opposite: someone we wouldn't expect would end up winning.

Photos this spread: VAM

One year, competition tensions at the studio ran especially high. My mom came in the night before the big day to remind me that results were subjective, meaning they'd be based on people's personal tastes and experiences. There are so many things people like and dislike that are outside of a performer's control. My mom gave an example: maybe one of the judges was hit in the head with a tambourine when they were little, and now they don't enjoy the tambourine dance.

The very next day at the competition, my teacher was accidentally hit by a dancer's tambourine backstage, and she had to have stitches!

At competitions, dancers usually get comments from three judges. It was interesting when I would get opposite feedback about the same dance.

I think people start to recognize you after a while, and it's human nature to like what you know. One time, I received a sought-after first-place at YAGP (Youth America Grand Prix). It was exciting, but I knew it was a little bit random.

We often spent a few days in January wondering whether we would spend our spring break at YAGP New York finals. When I got first place, I didn't qualify as a soloist, but I got to go to New York three times, including with a duet. It was inspiring to see so many amazingly talented dancers. The judges had a tough decision with so many standout performances. With dance, there are no check-boxes or scoring, so the results are always a little subjective.

It's not just competition dances that people have varied opinions about. My mom goes to see many dance performances, and she loves to ask people about their favorite dance and dancer. It's fascinating how everyone has different opinions about everything. She and I often agree on our favorite dancers, but many times, we don't agree on our preferred dance.

Photos this spread: VAM

It's similar with pictures. Ask a few friends which of these pictures they like best. I bet you'll get different answers, even when it's the same dancer. It's wonderful that we are unique and have our own individual preferences. We might even like a different picture tomorrow, because no two moments are the same, and even our own opinions change. If you've read our other books, do any of these poses look familiar?

Here are a few more pictures highlighting the ballet poses we'll learn today. On the top row is one of my favorites, *arabesque*. And since I've been thinking about how a good attitude in stressful situations makes things easier, I thought it would be fun to think about the ballet position called *attitude*. I'm told when I was young I ran around telling my family, "I have *attitude*!" while making the shape and laughing hysterically.

Attitude legs can extend in different directions. When we talk *fancy French* about our legs in relation to our bodies, we say: *devant* (to the front), *à la seconde* (to the side), or *derrière* (to the back).

Warming Up

It's a good idea to warm up your body and muscles before we try our ballet poses. Here are some ideas:

1) If you know some ballet basics, do *pliés* and *relevés* in *first, second,* and *third positions.* Then, for each leg, do five *tendus* each direction and five *passés.** (If you don't know these terms, simply bend and straighten your knees ten times, then run or march in place, lifting your knees extra high.)

2) Give all of your parts a gentle jiggle or shake:
   - your hands
   - your arms
   - your feet
   - your legs
   - your head
   - your shoulders
   - your back

3) Reach up high, then bend over and try to touch the floor.

4) Draw ten circles in the air using your shoulders as your paintbrushes.

5) Draw circles using each elbow as a paintbrush. Make five little ones and five big ones with each elbow.

6) Draw five little and five gigantic circles with each hand as your paintbrush.

Second position plié

*We practiced these dance moves in the first two Dancing Shapes *books.*

Part Three

Ballet Positions

I think the best way to start is to focus on our legs for a few minutes. Let's begin with some detail practice, thinking about the legs, feet, and toes.

Add in some turnout, meaning at least one leg rotates, or opens. With a turned-out leg, our knee faces out, and our heel comes forward. We rotate the leg as a whole piece, starting the open, or spiral, from the hip.

Let's repeat that last pose with the other leg.

Now that we've had a little brain-to-foot connection practice, we'll use it to think about the ballet position *attitude devant*.

Lie on your back, and put both legs up in a diamond shape. Rotate your legs so your knees face mostly to the side. Bring your heels as forward as you can while you keep your toes pointed. Double check that your back is straight and that your hips are relaxed.

Cross one foot a little in front of the other, keeping your foot shape the same. Use a similar leg position when you stand up and try *attitude devant*.

Attitude devant

Let's move on to our *attitude* side leg position. Try the sitting pose to find the knee lift. Stand up and hold on to something to find the standing leg position. Then add a pointed foot, and you have *attitude* in *à la seconde*. Be sure the hip of the leg in the air doesn't lift up farther than it needs to.

Attitude in *à la seconde*.

Moving on to the hardest one: *attitude derrière.* From our hands and knees, we reach our bent leg behind us in parallel by reaching our toes up to the ceiling. Then we rotate our leg to the side so our knee faces sideways while keeping the rest of the leg in the same shape. This is our *attitude derrière* leg position.

Next, we'll stretch our leg into a straight *arabesque* leg. You should still have a turned-out leg in the air and a parallel bent leg under you. Be sure to try both legs if you haven't already.

Once you've practiced those shapes, you could also try the *arabesque* and *attitude* legs with your hands and feet on the floor for a little extra practice before trying to balance. Start with both legs parallel and a little bent. Then straighten the bottom leg as much as you can and turn out your leg in the air. Finally, extend into an *arabesque*.

Try to stand up and find your *attitude derrière*. It might help you remember to keep your back up if you reach your arms up to the ceiling.

Attitude derrière

From *attitude derrière,* we stretch our back leg to create our *arabesque*. The standing leg should also be straight. We often see reaching, extended arms paired with *arabesque*. Here, my hidden arm reaches out to the side in a similar position to the front arm.

Arabesque

Part Four
Thinking About Details

Photo: Oliver Endahl/Ballet Zaida

I'd love to show you some additional poses and have you copy them. A few reminders from our other books to help you re-create these shapes:

- Some of these are really challenging. Be gentle with your body, and do what works for you.
- Think about each part of the body before trying to replicate the shape.
- Hold on to something, or work on the shape while sitting, if it feels a little difficult to try all at once.

Let's begin with some *arabesques*.

For an extra challenge, try to make the positions using the other leg.

We can use the same concepts of looking at whether our legs are turned out or parallel, and bent or straight as we add other elements to make more difficult shapes.

The positions on this page might not be possible when you first try them. Try lifting your hips just a little the first time, and then practice until you get stronger.

Again, no worries if these don't work at first. It can be fun to have a challenge and make small progress toward your goals. For your first try, make a smaller diamond or lift your head just a little off the ground.

We dancers get stuck in ruts where we often do the same arm-leg combinations. It's nice to challenge myself to create new shapes once in a while.

It's so tiring working brain and body. Maybe I'll hold my leg up, and then I'll just collapse on the floor. 😏

Remember that job I was waiting to hear about? It's been three days since they said they'd let me know, and I check my email every hour. Let's share this anticipation. I'll let you know in the next book whether I headed back to Boise, Idaho, or packed up to start over in Missouri. I bet I'm more curious than you, but this is how it goes, and I'm getting used to it. And who knows where I'll end up next fall? I might even be back in Seattle, doing my *attitudes* and trying to have a good attitude.

I hope your life is a little more predictable and that things are starting to get back to normal by the time you're reading this.

Keep practicing.

Keep trying to be the best you can be.

Be kind.

Until our next adventure,

Love,

 *Konora*

Photo: Oliver Endahl/Ballet Zaida

Fancy French*

- plié ['plee-AY'] bend (bent/bending)
- relevé ['rehl-i-VAY'] raise (raised)
- tendu ['tawn-DOO'] stretched (might also hear *battement tendu*)
- passé ['pah-SAY'] passed

(*passé* is the movement, *retiré* is the position, both words are used)

- retiré ['reh-tee-RAY'] withdrawn
- arabesque ['air-a-BESK'] a decorative pattern of intertwined flowing lines
- devant ['duh-VAHn'] in front
- à la seconde ['ah-la-say-KON'] to second (movement that goes to the side)
- derrière ['deh-REE-air'] behind

Bonus: penché ['pawn-SHAY'] leaning (pictured on this page)

Other Poses Mentioned

- first position
- second position
- third position
- attitude

Coming Up Next

If you know any young children, we've launched a series of Dance-It-Out creative movement stories for kids ages four to six. We've also started a fifth Dancing Shapes book and a series of three books for children ages eight to ten. Grown-ups can subscribe at *www.OnceUponADance.com*. (Watch for bonus subscriber content.)

*Not official pronunciations

Photo: VAM

This is our fourth book in the Dancing Shapes series. If you've read a few of our books, yippee! That makes us soar with joy! We are so glad you've come back, and we'd love to hear from you on Amazon or Goodreads.

Once Upon a Dance is a mother-daughter pandemic creation. While we wait to get back to outside life, every review, email, or comment fuels us during this isolation.

Breath Movement Imagination!

Dance-It-Out Creative Movement Stories for Young Movers

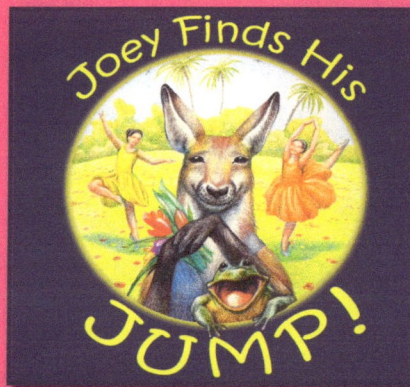

2021 Coming Soon:

Princess Naomi Helps a Unicorn

Brielle's Birthday Ball

Danny, Denny, & the Dancing Dragon

The Cat with the Crooked Tail

Danika's Dancing Day

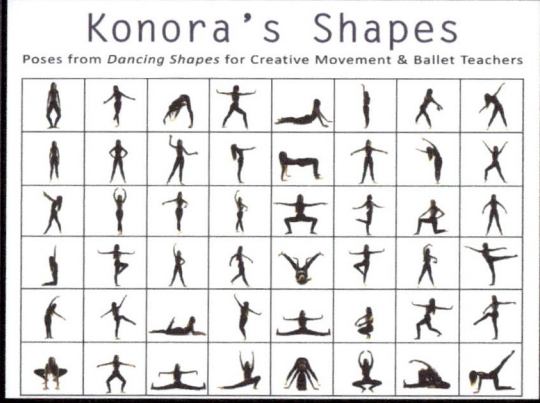

"Beautiful images and creative dance activities! I am so impressed with the quality and concept of this book series (this is our third). The images are crisp and beautiful and the ideas for using the book are SO MUCH FUN!

My kids (age 6-11) and I are having a great time trying out the activity ideas that go with the images…The activities are stretching us in many ways: dissecting and recreating poses down to the smallest details, using dance/movement vocabulary, teamwork, problem solving, thinking creatively, etc…"

www.OnceUponADance.com

www.ingramcontent.com/pod-product-compliance
Lightning Source LLC
LaVergne TN
LVHW070407080526
838200LV00089B/362